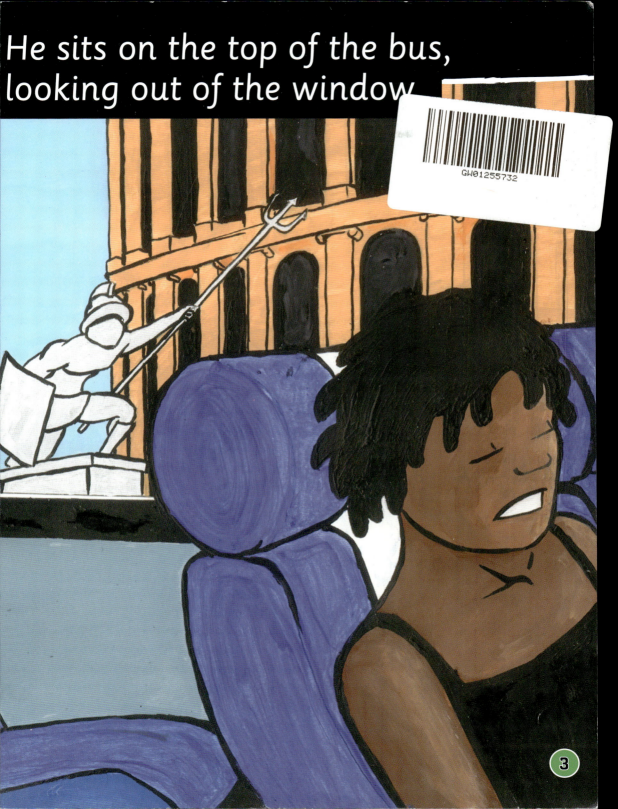

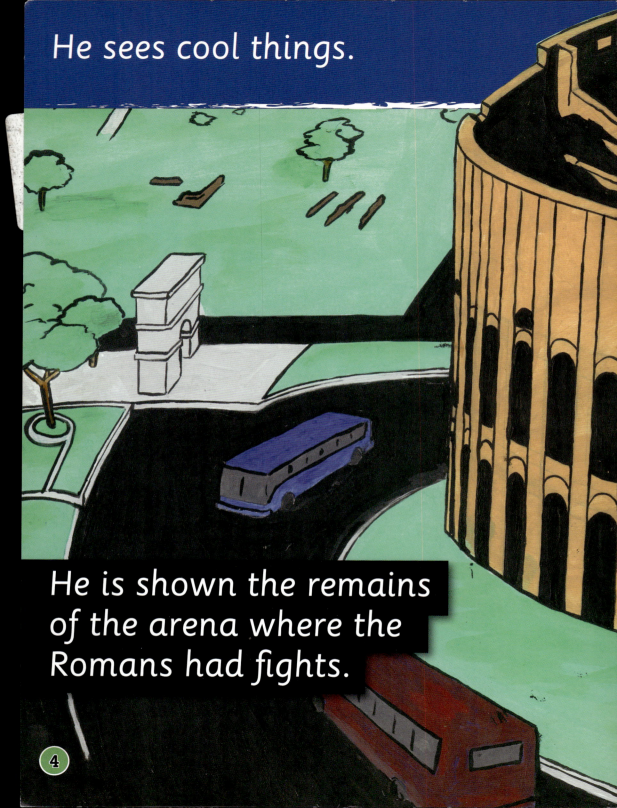

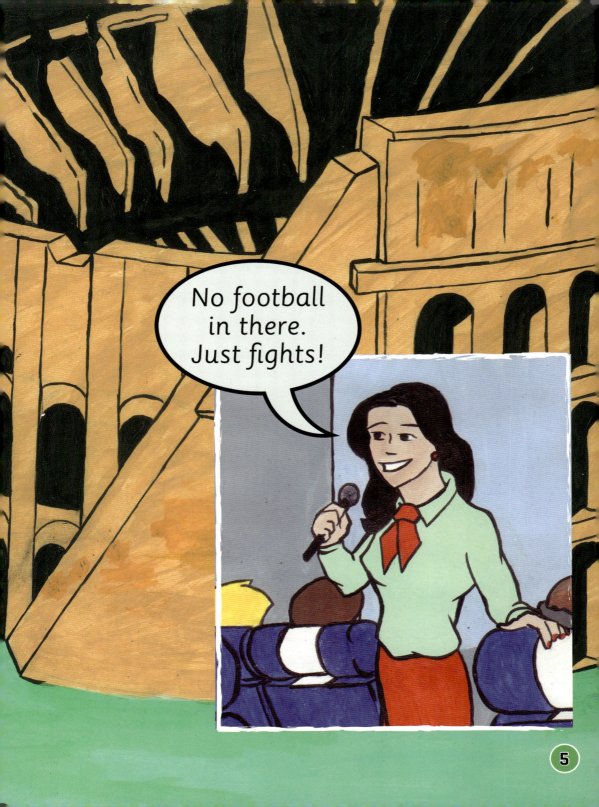

But Mark has been on the bus a long time, and it is hot. His head begins to nod and he soon falls asleep.

Quit pushing me.

Get out now! March to the doors!

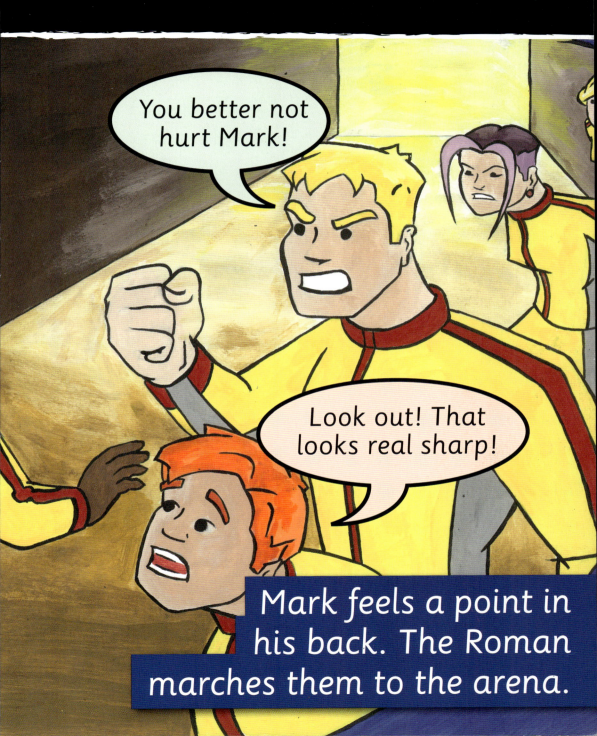

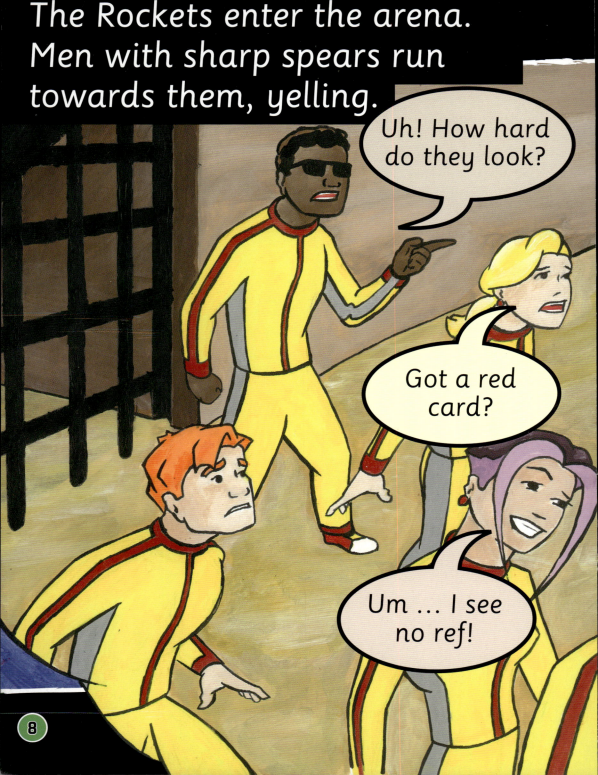

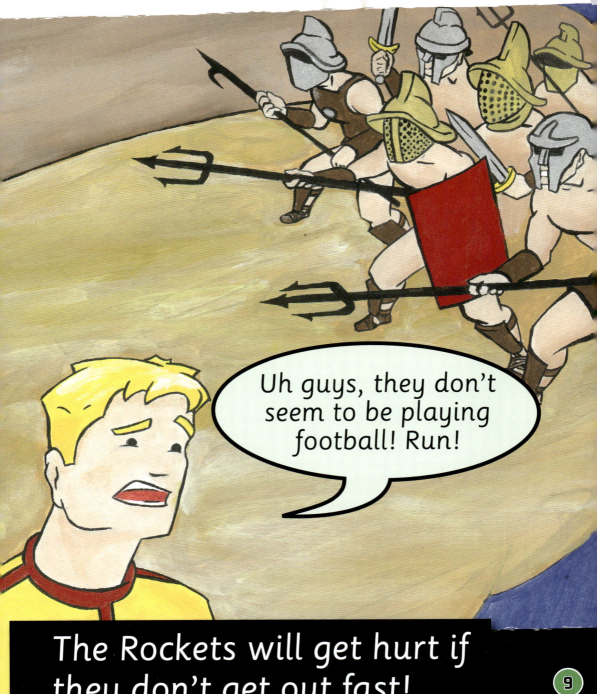

But Mark stops the panic and gets them all together to plan an attack.

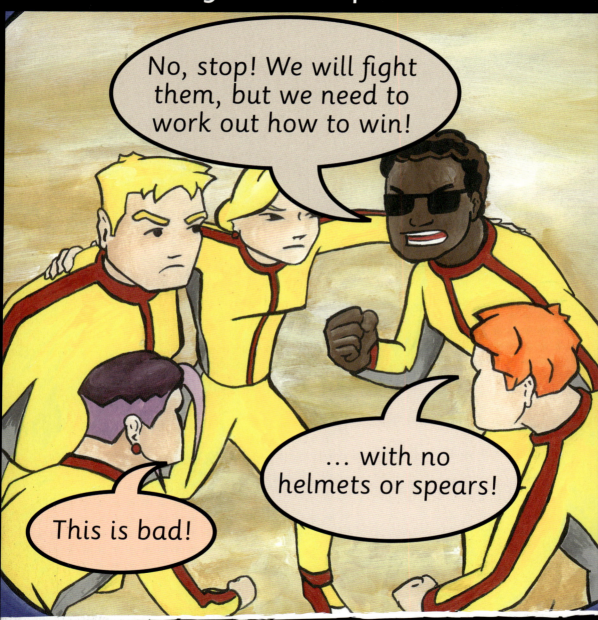

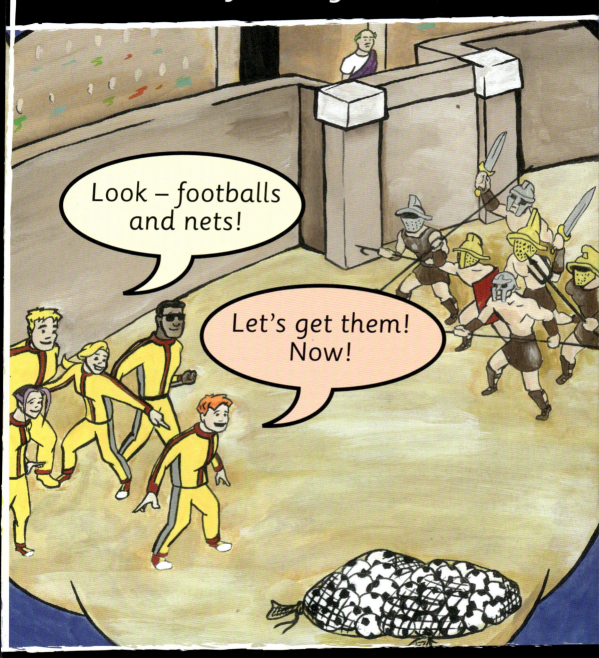

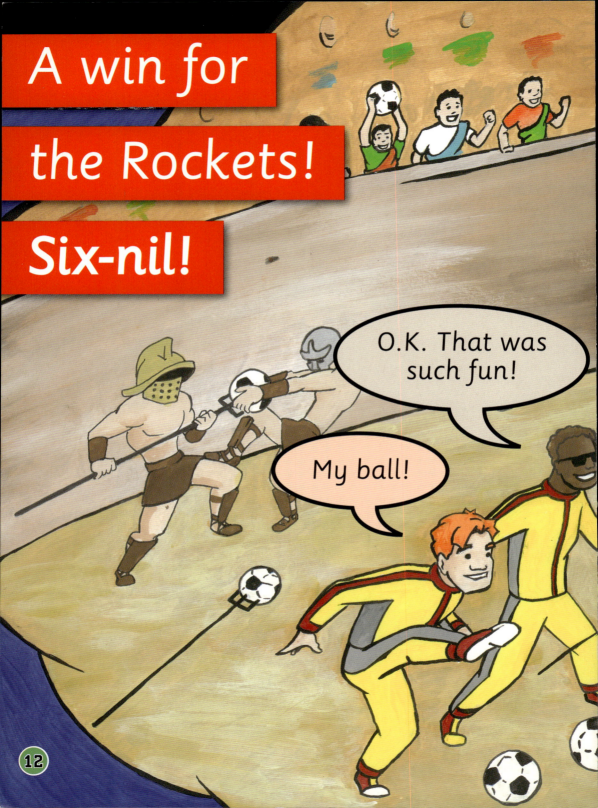

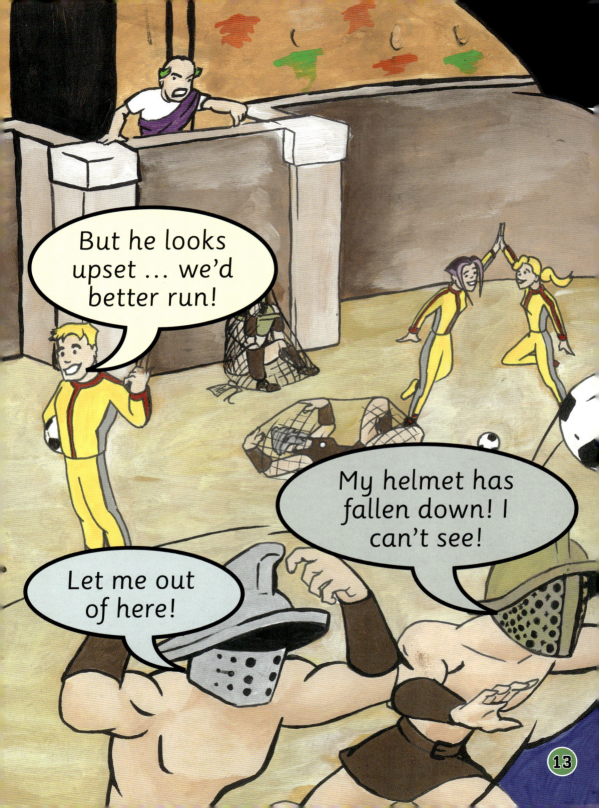

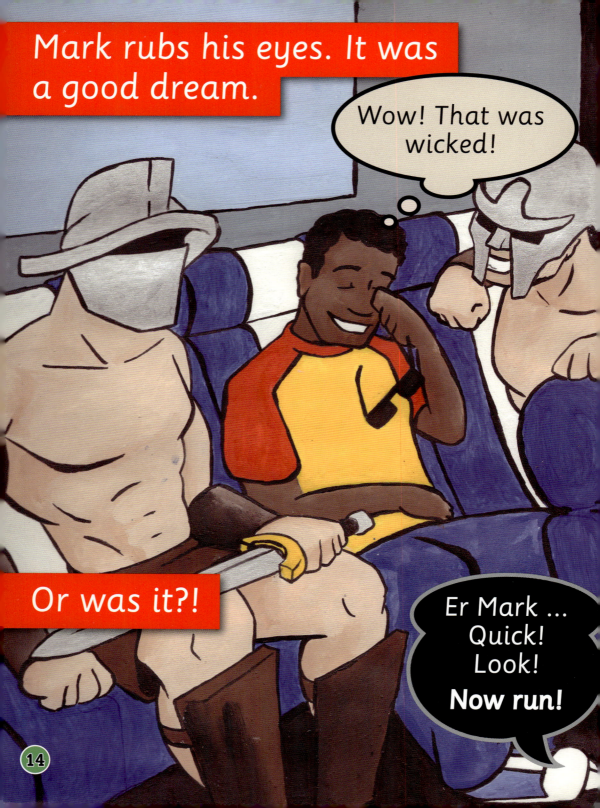